Saints and the World Left Behind

Sails the Wind
Left Behind

Alessandra Lynch

Alice James Books

FARMINGTON, MAINE

Grateful acknowledgment is made to the following publications in which these poems first appeared, sometimes in slightly different forms:

American Poetry Review: "Forecast," "Love Poem," "The Sound," "What We Impart"; *Columbia: Journal of Literature and Arts:* "Another Version of Insomnia," "A Sail the Wind Left Behind," "Black Robe," "Where I Live"; *Great Midwestern Quarterly:* "Away Near the Deaf Sea," "Wake"; *Hayden's Ferry Review:* "Making Conversation"; *The Little Magazine:* "Bullfight"; *Pegasus:* "I've Heard You Dreamt"; *Ploughshares:* "The Fly-Cage," "The Fight," "The Wedding to Black Garter or Trussed"; *Quarterly West:* "Dry Slats Against the Wind."

My thanks to the Vermont Studio Center for providing time to work on these poems and others. Thanks also to Cort Day, and love to my teachers, students, my family, my tribe.

10 9 8 7 6 5 4 3 2 1

Alice James Books are published by Alice James Poetry Cooperative, Inc., an affiliate of the University of Maine at Farmington.

ALICE JAMES BOOKS
238 MAIN STREET
FARMINGTON, MAINE 04938

www.umf.maine.edu/~ajb

LIBRARY OF CONGRESS CATALOGING-IN-PUBLICATION DATA
Lynch, Alessandra, 1965–
Sails the wind left behind / Alessandra Lynch.
    p.   cm.
ISBN 1–882295–36–6
I. Title.
PS3612.Y54 S25 2002
811'.6—dc21
2002004571

Alice James Book gratefully acknowledges support from the University of Maine at Farmington and the National Endowment for the Arts. ❦

Cover art: James E. Schuck, *The Way Out,* photograph, © 2002.

For my mother, mia bella mamma

Contents

III

THE FLY-CAGE

The cage is the only creature alive
singing in the yard
singing its giant heart out
singing its giant electric heart out for us.

We who have been the other's hour,
we who have made the minutes accountable
and the seconds lively and saw the big tree lovely,
we and our hands slowly fall
apart, heavy as damask.

We give no notice to the tiny fly-hands singed in prayer,
the litter of ash thumbs, the white butts
of their bodies, we will not note

their lives spent black and disturbed
as they hounded the dead and disabled and fell
passionately in love with cold-blood light
and screamed through the bars for it and could not
cease kissing its white lips
that so harmed them,
that would not reply.

I

WHERE I LIVE

I live in a village dull with perfume.
They call the bottle stalwart;
walls bow in
toward it,

windows blow out
of their dull minds,
but I live in a time
of a hill through fog and a train through the snow.

I live in a past passage of the rageful crow
and its stalkfirst feet;
it has staked my sleep
and forced me to crawl through flamethrown dawn.

I begin my day in slow burn,
the stove unlit and the flower's mouth stuffed
with bribecloth and weep.

I begin stacking wood in a miniature village
wearing the flint of wake and the stone of sleep.

I live in a sleeve of love which won't have me
leaning against moonhay which don't love me
strumming a stack-tune in three-fingered rain.

ARRIVING

I hear you, bells
I hear you, books
I hear the costly wheel creep close
to take a better look.
I hear you, fly,
on two thin hinds,
in sanctimonious squalor,
cant of rack and rhyme.

From acerb mouth,
from dark beads that compose a skull,
I hear your pant pant.
I hear you
from the pit
where I, unruly, turn
to shameless curl.

My lack of pure absence,
my visitation,
my inability to affirm or raise.
I hear you leaving through the front door,
stealing all my silver as you go,
taking the mirror, my face in it.

WHAT I ATE WHILE
YOU WERE AWAY

I was the scarf that ate the neck ragged.
Primarily, I wolfed the house of air.
(It tasted of grief and so I heaved.)

8 stop signs I ate;
the streets halted in amazement.
A reckless horse slowed to stunt-hoof;
wild chalk skid a burning blank.
(I ate, too, a few of caution, yield, and go.)
The green light's emeralds scorched my throat;
whereupon I ate a winter rose to recompose myself.

Then bent and ate the grainy inseam of the ant;
I licked the worm's sullen esophagus clean;
I ate the coal-fault and splurged on split diamonds;
I swallowed thick pride—the lion's mane still twitching
between my teeth.
(Now, eat the gloaming, I thought, you'll need your sleep.)

I ate the thought, but disregarded dreams.
I ate lug-bolt, cog, spur, then shunned the birds.
I hawked my way through parking lots to grovel and groove
on shards, rims, claws, and the spent rust of inelegant frames.
I stuffed my spleen with gravel and dusts
and staggered off.

FIVE O'CLOCK SUN
IN TALL GRASS

When the other world turns
the sky can't bear
its weight—

bruised cloud lowers
scraped by light
bones in flowery turf:

mangled daisies handcuffed to ragged sleeves
dark tarry iris—one eye filled

with violet smoke. You are not
alone or endangered
though you lie in beautiful, afflicted fields.

The five o'clock sun is your sister in the tall grass—
her scabbing golden leg idling in the weeds, her shadow lengthening

toward the irrevocable.
Daily she watches you unlatch to recount the primary within
a splurge of jewelweed, shivery iridescent fly-wing.

Untie yourself—
float, hover above
pale-armed lilies in the ember-mouthed river.

CHILDHOOD

Days we took our fathers down the path
to throw bone-white crumbs.
Days we crouched on the lower bank
to stare at our unspeakable images.
Days we led our fathers to the muddied
jut of the tacit stick.
Days we took our fathers to the swans.

Days we started from
the season's fall, the plummet of hewn oak,
the red lash of leaves, the ardent clash with wind,
wild ravagery of twigs, fierce skeletal scrapes,
plumage floating on the pond, dismantlement of swans,
total breakdown of woods.

Days we knew the muted beauty of the parks
and nothing of impossibility.

HEDGE

Long ago you buried father as one
would bury a hedgehog;
carefully, afraid that it was still alive
afraid that its pink, pinched face
would start screaming,
its spine rising
to dangerous heights,
but moon-sick
and amnesiac of spring,
its tail painfully thin.

It wasn't your responsibility, someone else had left him
on the road, his ribless side kicked-in,
fur—blood-dry and militant,
comical digits splayed, diligent to death.

Was the hill high and soft enough? Did it matter
the limited attendance, the lack
of funerary? (Even the wind
dropped out of the picture.)
Does it matter that the hill wouldn't flatten,
but huddled dazed and yellow?

Wandering over this mound, that mound,
it wasn't so long ago you buried him; you could have burned him
instead, could have scrubbed his bristle-fur
to shreds and fed him to the Hudson River whereon
razor-glints and pistol-butts, threadbare reflectives of a universe,
float. You could have been more decided.

It seems every corner we turn there is
another hedgehog, belly-up, mucous-crammed eyes,
toed to the side under copper-beech or oak.
(Once he listened politely to the names of trees
but really had no interest in anything
but burrowing.)

You're letting him lie
beneath the soil in full suit.
He might be alive—how shameful to dig him up again. Once
he told you *let the sleepers sleep and don't play in the dirt
and* ... you'll be walking hastily away

in case he rises and wakes
with a mouthful of soil, his hands tamped flat without the former
Herculean strength that lifted
the buried world and, single-handedly,
sloughed it off.

BLACK ROBE

What's to be pretty about?
A black robe of oil cast off in the drive.
A man who must rasp and has no say-so,
losing the voice that never was raised.
The knob tightens. A door looks away.
What put me up to this?
The meat drags on by string and hanky.
Blaze-bold headlines flatten.
So what's pretty?
Nostalgia is my pulse. The heart dons its mask.
Memory's faltering blinds skew both light and shade.
His tub huddles. His sink whitens and shrinks.
The chair, too, where last he sat.

What's to be pretty about?
A man who comes home in a box? The nth degree drops.
I dare this coldness—implement yourself.
These slippers scuffle back and forth upstairs
and will not descend.
Crutched bones hid in a new alarm of flesh.
These hands wondering what to do not first, not last, but then.
This face is too big for its stem.
This mirror too slight for the head.

The line of urns breathes when I look away.
This afternoon of long looks.
This lost year engaged to its routine mirror.
This ardent reflection without its reflector.

FORECAST

A rung, the silver wince of rib, a cutthroat shard, a fish-glint, a fib
that we have wings and fins and can swim anywhere
dragging behind familiar aluminum,
an uncradled family of pieces:

Even if

you were to abandon every ivory, green
morsel, blue jewel, eventually they will find you
where I've found you
in your yellow dress, wrestling the newfound
gravity of day, falling short of your shadow, wrestling
against hoods and death and a woman
who will not cast her eyes away from you, breathing iron grates,
stalking from tree to tree: hoarse flash/sooted satin
of crows, she is aiming to be
the brownest throat of forsythia
for a daughter who
in springtime cannot utter any word

but *forecast:*

Be an endless visitor
in star-spackled zenith, knee-deep in sky.
Say goodnight
to the blue, unsteady lips, the skin
of delphinium split by the end of spring, spilt
too soon from the milky stem.
Be not her daughter—
Not mine—

Yours,

LEST I FORGET

Let me record
the bluish lid of the moon—

it seems sick and old and ready to go—
no music in its blood—
no inward management.

Its one eye sits too still
in the middle of the sky.

WAKE

Here is the river of my poetry I run by every morning and note:
Here is the river of my poetry.

Horses have washed ashore, many in pieces:
white whinnying heads, four-leggedly;
houses, sodden as paper in a split of rain;
many roofs overladen by the sky
and its simple task of presenting stars;
many ineffective shards.

My love, pulling wagons of burnt oil and darts.
My love, filling lakes with limp-necked weeds.

We're exchanging flowers without roots.
Names buried deep in our fists,
we strike out, anonymous and dark,
to find the river
to tell it where it can't go, that it mustn't sleep:

Wake, do something, turn again to me.

SEA & STONE

"The last time we saw the fog together and remarked upon
our distant ship, you began to sink into the local lake—turning
iridescent, soon tucked in your own mudbank, a briny jewel hid
in your secret mouth, cattails in brownthroated chorus around you.

There, you were privy to the dropped feet of swans, privy
to flickering minnowdart, the lurking light of the drowned moon,
its underwater city of ghosts eddying, swaying with each deft
maneuver of water, whorling itself, snagging lilystems, rising,
   ducking,
dropping suddenly in a blur
of your private choreography—

you'd had a conversation with the sea
to learn about the ponds and moats that would succeed.
It was there I must have been
still wanting."

II

THE PLANET TONIGHT

(As if this planet were a cloud,
As if our light were enough.)

Some call the black glove dangling
without apology: *the night.*
Others have no name for what's unsparing.

Aching for another identity—
(Tiny scarlet tulip in the sky-black soil, dramatically
blistered mouth, flickery shimmy—
flame in tophat, sliding its slow foot
across the mirror, toeing the blue lake for a mothy shiver.)

it is the customary act—

(The curtain drops to earth
turning worlds to red velvet, burying
faces in astral dirt.)

to find faults within planets—

(Star-kicked fireflies will singe
their south, blotting along in loose knots over
the horizon.)

writing off shadows.

Darling, my grim line meets your fine sketch
while the world trembles below to think
of our happening this way without shields—
galaxy in palm, armfuls of dawn, praising the indefinable
light that people mistake for blood
leaking into the street.

A DARK HAT FOR
MICHAEL BURKARD

You do not say *light's wandering moon.*
You do not say *the bell hid its hurried face*
or *the heavy arm fell out of the tree again.*

Where are the grave rivers?
Where are the grave rivers that whip through heedless of the ice
they wrack? The forest waits patiently.

I crane the long neck around, I twist, I hunt for rope,
I glimpse the hanging weeds, the dragging lace of the sea.
I am at home nowhere and still the moon knows my address.

This is the steel knuckle in the fight.
This is the swift blow
that knocked the wits into the owl and the wits into the armchair.

The heart closes at its appointed time.
I wait like a dark hat
floating down the thin water of the river,
buckles broken, clanking against one another at boatside
and the belts lashing furiously out.

I want to tell the full story
but this is beside the point
You were the door, briefly letting visitors in and out.
You were the polite wing upon which I hung bodies weighted
with scrap, blackbird thievery, unraveling scarves
through which smokes inched themselves.

I am echoing the former
losses and your face looks up from another tired river
to tell me:

you don't need to claim another thing—this handful is yours—
your mouth, your gate, your house rising in the sinking storm.

SHIRTS

None are sleeved; one a comic tunnel-eyed
mouse with a breezy smile, one marooned, darkening
at the collar, hollow.

Strange like mouths all twisting to speak,
heaped: dark and shirred like fish, bleach-puckered
brine-stained. I do not expect gifts

'or know how
to receive. Waifs of cloth, light hefts

bereft in the box, anonymous, new
without personhood: none
guilty, none covering

me entirely,
no Daisy-silks—flimsy
surrogate limbs aswim—weep of flotsam

that might have tied around me in the night or pinned
their naked weeds to the headboard, my hands
like floating carp, my face pressed for your smoky blur.

Will these shirts hold
me, barely by a hem? Will their loose
oversized—eager threads—
warm or harm?

The grinning mouse again—plastered large as a pirate sail
against my small-hulled chest, flattened against ridiculous ribs
that barely hinge themselves, my smallish

left breast hanging out,
furious berry of a nipple squinting at the mirror
desiring you here. Emerge. Walk behind me

in the glass—cup one hand
like a cracked blindfold
over the breast. Be my hidden partner.

Look closely with me: watch the flesh
shimmer in the glass

where the heart would be trembling

if the sleeves had been filled with arms, not air.

REWIND

In the hotel room we outdid Hopper:
I did not sit on bed-edge, grime-lit;
you did not bury your head in the papery lampshade;
I did not strut fiercely with red nipples and a sneer;
you did not turn into a floral chair.

In the hotel room we painted the moon with a single hair,
then walked crookedly straight into each other, naked
through the stop-sign mirror, through the black forest of the past
where we lay like two cobalt-blue oars breathing;
our proudish musculature lured movingly by rivers welled up.

Outside—the cracked crate of the heart
sits in the branch with silent hands
as the skin of the river floats off
as the dusk of our sound settles dark.

THIS IS WHERE YOU ARE

This is your sill. White
out. Out of the picture. This
is my foot. Once. In your mouth.
On your rug. In your crotch.
This is my picture. Not
where you are. Not docile
snow. Not obedient
rain. This is not sun
down. This is not twilight. This is
not my favorite place for illumination.
This has little bearing on cloud. This is
not the high tower where we work
our hearts on clothesline. This has
no mercy.

Is this the bird Stern
told me to write? Is this the poem he
told me to write? About birds. He said
protect the green stone. Protect
the marigold. He said protect the iron
link fence and the tall breath
of ceilings, the rose firewood, the shabby
soft brick. He said stand by your walls
no matter how shrunken the stone. No matter
how cheap the cement. He said don't drop
guard. Wear a gun. Effect moss.
He said watch out for the ice man has planted.
He said they're all bad (trying to unravel the shrill
chicken skin that is always ours that we do
not love or cannot love while saying we do).

Protect yourself, he said.
(In two words he tried to dispel bad
loving.) Did he swear by them
through the wine and fish and strawberries
when they lurked the skullock table,
when their pale wind wracked the sumac
and dashed the few birds I'd handled?
Did I?

We hadn't even the cracks
of a heart to feed, not
a trickle. (No breath left to spell
any name. Let alone ours.)

YOU ARE NOT THE WOLF
IN MY ROOM

though you filched a rainbow, bent its elbow back until it spoke
and became a wheel for you, wheeling you wherever you wanted;

though you wrung a wild tree sick
and ordained it for fire;

though you goad and spit the cloud
to ruined fur, slack with mud.

The blue axe you loved and stroked
you abandoned to the maw of blade-starved rust.

Skeletal as keys, I caught
you sleeping with a porpoise wearing a white wig,

and envy caved my face
that wears a bride's masked smile.

Erase you, erase you not.
A flower halts its stemmy step before you,

bent in thin concentration as you pin
and crucify childhood's lizards.

REMIND ME

Remind me to tell you about candles that ate through
my hair, leaving lace in my eyes
and the red-winged blackbird's assault as she wrestled
my friend in an Iowa ditch.

In love with rivers and out again—
in love with rivers.

Remind me to tell you which was my saddest river,
which river hid beneath the bridge,
which river hurried breathlessly around the bend.

Let us remind one another
we have messages to deliver:
one to the father and one to the father's son,
one to the sinking hillock and one to the cock's harsh disregard
one to the window, raped of its curtain, exposed to bare light
one, soft-lit, to snow
one, soft-lit, to night.

Remind me to remind you to
let in the wind that shoves out the cold
and blasts the bird blind.

CLAUDIA,

the idea of a cloud drifting over
the garden, an auditory azalea
loud with light, Claudia, the wind
lifting heft and hem of the fence for a town
of wild astronauts and August's wrought roses,
the only memory cloistered in my amnesiac field, Claudia,
cloisonne of cloverweed and woods staggering deep—
the clearing life we led is strictly memory; the rest, the every-
day drags us coastward—slow symphonies badly conducted.

Claudia turns and kisses the strings, embraces the baton,
the keys that lock us deftly in: lends a brace
of darkeyed doves, feeds the empty swing with grace
still swung. Claudia, one more minute to darkness
a second more to slip into the slit
of your serious eye, your dedicated sight
and considerate sands, the cloud you up-hover, shift—
the us you coalesced, my oldest love.

MAKING CONVERSATION

"Maybe if the blue moon listened more
closely to the red moon,
it wouldn't spend days crouched
under a blizzard of barbed wire,"
I said as we struggled along like yaks,
the snow up to our throats.

We hauled horsemeat and seawater;
butterfly ashes; a pearl's abdomen;
clouds of dust from fugitive heels;
We lugged our heavy contents.

You didn't look at me. You were afraid.
Your mind occupied by an eyelash, a stray
that fell into the driver's eye on a blind curve
and halted all sound. I wanted to speak lightly,
but the snow was closing
its leadweight door.

We were two shaggy-haired yaks heading towards the woods
where a bruised piano waited under a meek sky;
the moon's chin sunk on the key of D.
Even here, the wind bullied and cleaved
the snow. "Isn't it time we rest?" I asked you
as we hit the forest and labored through the shadows.

This is an old, beautiful, deadly story.
The snow is a seductress.
If we paused here, we would fall into her dream,
frozen, two mouths fed on winter grass.

LOVE POEM

I stopped the Ask
in its track.
It drew a long claw through the snow.
It was a mute dart,
fatal in the pillow.
Before long, it became a dream.
Everyone walked off,
relieved.

The sun shelved itself in the dust.
I lived in a closet and ordered the hangers out.
Windows broke in the night, neglecting their frames.
Doors, lanced through the jamb, lost their swing.
I stopped the Ask from crawling from its casing.
I stop the Ask again.
It turns into a watch that ticks, that sees

the one life of my love walking slowly
from the pier. I loved his walk,
his consideration for the weaker planks,
the struggling nails bent at their necks, his respect
for the huge silent children hunched over the rail,
dangling their wires down, hoping to hook a gill.
I loved his quiet slant when he took
his fingers to my jaw, pried open the mouth,
and didn't start from what he saw.

A USUAL TALE

I.

We were two young dunes on a drifting
street in the threadbare rain. Sidled
from the stranger's living room
where the dangerous sea was caught in a bowl,
where the rest of the sea was lost in its looseness.

Blind-tight, tide roped us,
held us in. The sands frayed. We grinned and grin and grin.
I execute a savagery I cannot speak.
A shark brandishing its cutthroat tail I cannot catch.

II.

The fish lie sick.
The fish lie stink-sick at the bottom of the bowl. My own sunk

hand gloats white. Jewelfish float by
the half-smiles of silver hooks. My face
is a dark mask I left on the fin of a tree
undersea, undersea

where a dropped bell—the bell I dropped—
dove, dumbed.
Where every sound is kin.
Where all the sounds are kind. They cannot tell.

WHAT WE IMPART

So, you vaulted the back of a deer as it plunged into the river.
Was that a confession?
Was it a gloat? Was it the splintered
glass of your spirit? Was it a mothy scrap to be stuck
by memory's tack into amnesiac's spine?
Was it a comment on your powers or failures? Was it a wire
with another message attached, hung loose as laundry—reeled up
to the invalid? Was it a window
glaring out from its frame to the exposed south?
Did you really intend to tell me or did it slip out, shocked
by its own clang? Was it a bell chime?
Did it hiss? Was it the thick rattle of the marriage veil
as you kissed her cheek? Did it forewarn?
Was it a wistful sigh? Was it a start?
Did it ever clear its throat?
Was it a horror? Was it a sorrow? Was its blackly heaving
accordion a celebration? Should I have screamed?
Should I have shot a stone in the spine of a runaway arrow?
Should I have bottled us both with a ship?
Should I have held your hand?
Should I have vaulted my own?

WAS DRUNK

In the golden fields of Meadow Pond Elementary,
our favorite rebel game was drunk:
two bandits running to the far edge of the field
so no one would see us
losing it in the tall grass near the electric fence
that barely kept us in—a thin hair pin
for a topple of hair—bound to be loosed.
We'd stagger and tumble, fall and scream,
laughter punching our remarkable bellies out
under the tired sun—the other children far off—
in frozen punctuation
swung on their customary swings, docile in the sandbox
as we'd indulge in secret revelries,
imbibing the gold swoon of the wind
tipsy in the turning fields, we'd swagger
through saloon doors, barely able
to breathe for all our reckless delight
like twin bees hooked on honey,
our young breaths thick with yarrow-gin.
While, on the other side of the world,
you were already there, serious, posting your elbows
on mahogany, pounding down amber, barely able
to think about the meadow as it browned and spread its lavender
while we called to you from our fields
almost audible.

NEXT DOOR

His heart stopped by a fly,
a quiet man lies in the desert.
Sand fills his pocket.

The family's shadow drifts
from desert to wood.
The family knuckles in next door.

Mutely grouped, their lawn chairs sit out-
side all night.
All night, bloodroot blooms.

Berries' hunched faces continually darken.
Skin of eucalyptus tightens.
The front door sags in increments.

A tiny whine
rewinds the air—a tiny whine.
They keep an engine running in the yard.

The thin mother's a veil
drunkenly wandering in extol of twilight;
her daughter heavied dull water last fall;

her mad son cranks up his sleeves, listening to the gas-
meter's rise and shriek and will not, despite the calls,
turn down his music.

THE WEDDING TO BLACK
GARTER OR TRUSSED

Lump of vein
Rack of lamb, the lame leg—
today—a wing apart
from the central thing.
I find I found
and off the ground O, O awful
news. I've feathers
and no lift.

CONFESSIONAL, I

sought night, I
devoured a plateful of navy
thready with errant ink, I
tore the riverlily from its lilac root, I
kissed the sun's cracked meat without
love, caged my feet in bittersweet, I
locked the dog in the engine room till
it softly expired, pushed my brother over
the snaking bannister down
the stairwell till his skull met slate,
slipped between twilight rooms, witnessed
the father's protruding
fleshy nudity and the mother's absent sail, I
sought night, I
shifted restless, I was a wailing desert, dry with scorpion-leg
and mythology. I sniffed the brine-dust of stars, serious dunes
limped into my night, my family of infidel bones
drifted through
on their ragged raft, ransacking lakes
of chartreuse, my womanhood
dissembling as chalky grief: one moment
a mouthless mask, the next a rain-darkened cane leaning
on wind, barely balancing
its cloud. And when she finally became
invisible, I forgave her
for not bearing.

RED DOOR

Before they knew what was what, she painted the front door
red: whistle-red lipstick red STOP the scream of a cardinal's wing
a target in the woods
mocking the cloud-hung, clay-cold days.

Soon after, the vacuum sulked in the corner
and turned mute,
the dog lay quiet in the towering, soft grass
its ribs accusingly jut.

This is when they began the game of locking each other out:
brother to sister, brother to brother, sister to brother
their owl-bruised eyes peering out at the outcast or in at the inmate
testing to see how long they could last—
how long could their bare hands withstand the headlong snow?
—all the lowered lashes of the rain
the flagellant sleet—
how long could the heart stop short its cold turnstile
preventing their brethren from passing through

the red door she'd painted
that didn't belong, and little belonged
behind it.

BULLFIGHT

There'd been a bullfight in the house.
Four black eyes stared sullen from the range.
You weren't sure what hit how hard.
Your mother's lips pressed tight to a rose.

Your father, matador, menaced for her kiss. She led
him through night's scalded ring. He dazed her
with the flip switch of his knife. Their tight eyes gleamed.
You weren't sure who hit, but flattened in. Your father

came so close you heard his chest hair scream, caught
in the sidelong jaw of the zipper. He jammed her in
the sagging belly of the gas stove till she sank,
a soft flag on the floor. He fell too, a gored bull.

They lay like this all night, sick bulks, slaves,
beasts exhausted from the crawl and haul.
You weren't sure what hit and left them
there. You crept to where your mother hung

a man dressed in blood above her bed, his feet cross-nailed,
looking tired and pale, looking down on you.
His hands' limp petals flapped from skewed wrists,
old drapes wrapped his naked legs around. The torso writhed.

You weren't sure how hard they'd hit,
but had to walk far from that house, talking low
to the dirt you stepped on,
silent dirt dragging you in.

DRY SLATS AGAINST THE WIND

I.

With the lip of petunia out-stuck, frozen to a primary vein;
with not wanting here nor there,

I woke with the root of a coldblooded killer bunched in my hands,
the neck-veins of a fighter, pulsed, and the small eyes of a bull.

My heart sewn with coarse thread to the pillow's bleached skull,
The yellow bedside branch goffed urn-fallow water,

and so enlisted 7,000 stumps to walk with me and the blade
into dustpan dusk and its monotone day.

II.

Anger, you are always in danger.
Your wings hunch like dark hoods
frozen by a shivering river and a pinched star,
by the blare of an hour and a city's sullen horn.

No marrow-silk to your bones.
In the workaday world, no body to your flesh.
We speed secretly through marvelous nights,
intoxicated on the velvet tilt and lean of undulant trees
past the intermittent shutters' dry slats against the wind.

Be in hiding with me.
I will take you through every continent—
we will admire the silver-rimmed spade,
deep-taloned rake, sterling-barbed rains.
We will lie awake in a glistening field of knives
and open our hearts.

GLORIA SAYS

good is a thing i cannot touch
or hear   i cannot sing   voice not
rust but its color/ broken oriole   (gloria
flattens like yellow
finch on the welcome mat scruffed
fur on dog's dead back)   *i don't want to scratch*
or wash   i am this unscrupulous   (gloria
says)   *i am the hard, north tower & its hampered mouth*
filled with blue-dart flies & dagger-birds
gloria is that good, grief-struck end of the river
in the good air & its handful of asters & nasturtium (not answers)
in the good air's mouthful of lark (not lament or language)
not barbed letters (that cage us from the birds)
not electric spit   but marigold
copper hornet   bee-torn sky   interrupted

blues   gloria: grief is a noun i did not name
or pronounce   my fingertips dissolve
when i try to touch   its silvery issue
sons & daughters i have known   hiss
& spark like dark rivers addressed by the stars
which will leave them little
brightness   (would rivers that dark claim?)

(if good were the whole word, if good were as solid
as its sound, if good were as stout & clearly visaged
grief would've shrunk, cornered)   gloria & i

would not be wearing our nightmare faces   we would be
tearing the stuffing from our sleeves   we would be
kissing our endless angels   unbruised by the inky ravens
that darkened our dark longing   we would be
in good with good & out of grief   wouldn't we   wouldn't
we be wearing long white nightgowns fiercely
kissing each other's bad   burned mouths

TRAIN

All light's a dullard's now.
Our picnic's done.
Its carcass of grapes lies between us.
Tiny skull-seeds bitterly thrive.

We cradle the deadweight leg that will walk off,
reconstruct the splintering night,
love the unthawed snake that lies central in the road.

If only we'd had the swiftness of passing trains.
If only, coldly shuddering by,
we'd passed on the hairpin track.
If only we'd had one crux-eye shearing the dark,

our clean flanks clanking the gin-smut world,
after-smoke caught in a strangle of trees,
as we roared through the glazed rain and mute sky,
burnt out, the jingling iron frame,

a spark, a daub of oil, the only left-behinds.

THE SYLLABLE

Words lain
lovely as the necks
of swans browning
in the swollen river.

At last cry,
where is the frank acuity?
A stony throttle.
A quiet high-wire.

Scientists still don't know
why our world is dark at night.
She dreamt when she looked down,
she couldn't see herself.

No more sentiment.
No sparrows.
The thick grass of tomorrow
is stifling the short grass today.

Several million petals creak into flower.
A whole rose lies untouched, throbbing in the street.
I've given the dog my dinner again.

THE SAIL THE WIND
LEFT BEHIND

for Kirt

He didn't fight. He put down his fork.
For this, I don't blame him.
He took his time pulling on socks.
He paused between doors.
For this, I don't fault him.
He waited out his scale in the calm
house overshadowing the woods.
The dog was kind beside him,
stirring only when he stirred.

Birds closed their throats.
Black rags clapped vigorously, haplessly
for him to move on, move on . . . .

The continent within bunched and froze.
The sea's wet velvet tore.
For this, I drape the painting with a shawl,
unhinge the candle from its light.

The blue robe not handsome without him.

III

THE HOUR I WAIT FOR YOU

Can we only hold so much? Give me
hold onto the deeper eye. I will climb under your lid,
I will slip through the lash,
into the mirror. I recommend
we give ourselves over to darkness,

drain our wells
to recover, bait
midnight with cold meat. The hour I wait
for you, I wrong the birds, I wrong the brainstorm sleep
and infume the sky.

I want to be led into another
life, under another sun. I drop
myself for someone else to find, return to you.
How faintly I come home.

The hour I wait for you
is a hoax.
It is the hour
I love.

THE SOUND

in memory of Kirt

Nine poets born and one
steady drip.
It might be the sink or toilet;
blood from the ear, a blue snail wending and
cooling its twilit trail—the lips
of leaves or slap of the swallow
heading toward mud.

It could be the clock of the dying man.
Is it the tap of high heels
descending?
Is it the empty reel of the movie
clacking?
Or the invisible tool
nailing and prying each power line?

It is the threat of the neighborhood,
the smacking mouth beneath the thief's mask,
the twitched eye, doom. It ushers in
the still. Remnant

of man half out of bed, his gaunt
slipper caught on the iron fret,
his blood missing a vein,
his sail scant, too thin for all the wharf's wind.

Is this the drip of pipes, the drip of what
we've made our masterwork?
Does it forward the night?
Is that the sound?
Does it save?

BLOODSTONE

for Peter

He thinks he's found
a morning jewel: maybe ruby,
a red *eureka*—moved by vibrancy he stops
culling pebbles and dust for the scarlet
glint. It's a little heart-
shaped stone, a trickle of fresh blood
new on its skin, but there is no indication
of dragging tracks, no speaking witness,
no robin-lung fallen tiny in the grass
no corpsed tongue gashed by stoplight
glass, no tail shriveled to a string dripping
the mystery blood. No mangled finger bones.
Not a human sign. Still, he won't drop the stone
back into the hole it made. He grips its ruddy hold and turns
home—back to his easel, facing the eastern light,
the stone in his bare palm. He smears
canvas with its blood, foregoing
paint-choked bristles of the brush.

By dusk, Peter has sewn
a thread of marrow through its middle,
hooked a vein's dark shackle to the mirror,
kissing bloodstone while it dries, eyes
fierce-closed for crimson, lips
faint streaks of autumn.

FUSES QUICKLY SCORCHING
TO TAIL-END

We qualify as unnoted
bends in stony river
(mute dials buried) blue
threads, throats of the desert.

Still, the field slips between
us. We momentarily calm
eternity with torch, vermilion, plentiful
rooks and orioles. Squatting
under the bridge, squandering
our light for cover, we regard
steadily the ripped, lustrous flesh
of the thunderstruck river
the lower water gliding
in violet shrouding the fantail fins, weeping emeralds
jammed down with fur and feather.

We've spent lifetimes listing sparrows—
how delicate their birdwalk across
our hunched or broken
radiant spines!

WHAT THE MEADOW SAID
AFTERWARDS

meadow said *spring*
meadow could not hear itself think for all the bells ringing
meadow could not look to see whether the sun had turned blue
or the cloud became gold—meadow could not taste guttered wheel
nor sludge-barrow, nor sullen hill, nor blood-licked tin
that lanced asters to sorrel and lace to loam

meadow could not receive footfall
it could only feel rain and inward it turned
on itself for not having known
more

meadow said *drown daisies drown*
their obedient necks sodden green
their ridiculous twist-off faces
their petals falling like poor hats

meadow said:
be dead, heart
be the raft cracked
don't function as door
spill like salt, effortless, daft,
white-faced, aghast

choose the city in lieu, lying
removed, stiff with lights, crippled by wire, over
the sweet, dying blossoms, the stalks terrified
of their thorn.

DAMAGE III

For Red

The beaten speak of damage
with pinned mouths
and pin their images of the world in the hallway—
a slapdash smile, parade of oil drums, her thin calves
in sand, a naked convergence with driftwood, salt-bits
on the anklebone, traffic lights working their raw mouths,
slight yellow sobs, tremor of red eye.

The shadows from the street crawl out of their glint-dusty skin
into the tall rooms of the afternoon,
candles pry the wall
which has listened for a decade.
Pieces of light from the eyelets
of unlaced shoes pule through air
like white-throated sparrows
fusing blue sprigs to clouds,
trying to remedy surfaces with surfaces
or evoke kinship with sky.

The beaten are a blue mix of terror and asters, particular
about flavors and sounds and flames, plugging their damaged
ears, bandaging insular veins, filling famished floors
with wires, seedlings, rain.
They have been the central whorl of the whelk and the soft
bruise of the lid at its close.
They have been waxen as night-bridges, stiffly ridden by restless
lights and lost, creeping through galaxies of loose ends, seeking
strings and hangers they could

bend to open doors, unleash cats
from their tender napes, unknock
the shudder from the raw
knees cramped on slashed marble, bent double
from silence and flicker.

I am waiting for their will to unfold—
disperse solitary issue.

Again, I am leaning into them, I am tilting
my cave into their heat.

ANOTHER VERSION OF INSOMNIA

The cloud calls me from my stranded willow.
The owl calls me from the flaming glass.
The ant calls me from the broken-mouthed magnolia.
The sky calls me from its dragging tail-pipe.
The harsh peacock calls: *thin feather, blue tether*.
The lighted window calls shortly, then turns cold.
The rain that once touched it slinks off on an oil-drum downriver.
Now, every star is stapling itself alive
to any scrap of velvet it can find.

ABOUT THE STAR-NOSED MOLE:

it refused to be bedded in a poem
with the bull and hedgehog.
It refused to be the wolf in my room
and, moreover, would neither weep nor live
a third life. It would not even take
to the soil, however pushed to earth.
It was not fuel for the spade, it would not dangle
from precipice or burrow to birch-root and oak-sweat.
It would have no visitors and could not be
visited.

A mole
in a clench of dirt
(no air)
close to you, folding and unfolding the earth beneath you as you
covet what's other, what's not
and no breathing, no
forests, no imploring fist or foot,
no aster-shackled hill, no, not withstanding what it, no, not
endured, no man, not gripped like that, no how
no steam belt, no belly of dun, no rapture, no flame
no silken hide, no velvet
to claw, no ride
no ride out from my stuck self
there in the flowerpot
behind the picture plate
by the swinging seat
and its bruised slats
and its ditch.

I'VE HEARD YOU DREAMT

I've heard you dreamt of your beautiful mother
and her laughter
and language and could not speak
to ask her really
if she was alive for you or dead as assumed.

I've seen the wood on your mantel carved
by her fingers, slender as rivers.

I've seen the face of her smiles
and touched the deep-toned gloss of piano
and heard of her house in the woods
where wild snakes were welcome
and the blue-edged black butterflies flew with ease.

I've seen you rest your chin on the palm of your hand
holding it as though therein was the fortune
and misfortune and the gravity of whole planets
that spun and sparked in collision, but never stopped
defying the definite.

VASE

Even the bottom
of the vase is a long drop
down from where I'm sitting—rim-side
looking into
the dark tongueless mouth—

daisies and tiger lilies jut out: I should be proud
to be so close to them,
but their arms are severed and their glamorous heads
are evasive, gone to seed, not an ounce
of rageful thorn or sad tuft to hold
and their feet have been lopped off and dangle above
the bottom dropped out
beneath them.

Rumor has it that the whole vase
is yowling hollow and yellow
water seeps its reliable base and its clown's
jowl droops to soft ceramic and the flowers
will forever bend low in fruitless staggering
though I've heard it at midnight singing:

call into me for an echo—
that's when I tiptoed out
and aspired
to hit rock bottom, stone, slate, bone
bottom. I walked the city streets in bare feet
stepping on all the shards
in their brilliant lustre
mid-conversation with the stars—

till the opera singer steered steel
into my voice, drove me over the bridge and crooned:
come down to earth: drink soup, take a bath.

One night in a flood I felt how close my skin
was to the other galaxies and how no matter how
closely I approached the world
it would tilt or turn away.
(The night the echo knocked first
and floored our flowers,
I met gravity.)

INFLUENCE

Currently, I am rethinking my kiss of the dark road
and my haughtiness toward the dripping faucet:
lakes and lagoons wade up to me
deposit their silver
without syllable.

The particular music
behind the smoky door
has moved me
to put down the broken blinds
gauntly bent to hang,

to abandon the project of aligning the stars.
It seems to have snapped the wire
between me and the fattened moon.

ILLUMINATION

The gasoline ghost of a swan
drifts by—one blue-veined eye closed against
the too-bright world we have made in fear
of losing face.

I will not lose face tonight; I will blind
all lanterns, candles, bulbs
and sit in the dark,
watching clench-faced bats
drop, diverting twilight,
watching the jury rule out lives.

Isn't that what those with faces do?
Those with faces like widows hoarse with silence
and dog-sick of complaint,

their yowls snagged on a branch, never reaching Echo Lake,
their terrors tucked methodically as a spade
under a spoke,
trying to excavate the wheel.

The moon peers at me through the west glass.
Through the east glass; the whip-smoked tail of the comet,
and through the north glass—slow traffic,
and through the south glass—my face caged by wires and pipes,
cup-boarded.

The moon that effaces
is back again—
throwing its light over the street
cramming its white coal into open sockets.

REQUIEM

The news walks down
Its gangplank.
Slight veins unevenly bleed.

Twilight has shed all that was soft.
The blue hills feign sleep
Waiting for trains
To shackle to oily claw
And clouds
To strangle, blown like unwashed russet blossoms
And bridges
To buckle under blankly
And children
To scare from windowsills, turning
Into burning birds
Skidding across the highway.

What is the sky we deign to apprehend?
Where is its notion?
How can we direct ourselves? How navigate
The cringing bed-sheet, the hollowed shirt? What
To hang? To fold? What portion of this bread,
Which water do we take? Where is the strategy
Of laughter? Who stole the tactics of the lake,
The clear steer of wheels, the prophecies of fog?

Every chalk we touch
Is erasure, smoke reduced,
Hardened to fit
The unredeemable hand.

Our arrows glance off—
Sleek swallows, hoodlum minnows, the eastern
Sweep of rain through silver towers.

The dark is under
Renovation, has stilled
The invention of hours,
Leaves our moonlight alone
At road-hem, no
Drop left in the drained eye,
In the edgy puddle.

Somebody's grief, struck blind.
A cane pokes for substance
In the middle.

We are naked candles conversing with shadows.
Somebody needs location. And language. And a name.

A TURN HERE, A TURN THERE

I have a song the wind reels in—
a turn here, a turn there,
spelled by the moon, carried by air.

Wind, be my contemporary, not the enemy of sound,
emulate an ink-stained blossom,
wrestle a mountain from the folded ground,

lower me down where crystallized tongue
of whelk and whale
reside, slow and calm.

Wind, be my accomplice, torture the stone with a flame.
Blindfold the blind
Drum the deaf ear hard—it won't answer today.

I have so envied the dead
who walk pigeon-toed through a scuffle of doves,
who break the little skulls of pebbles, unafraid
of ordinary day.

The unassuming
hum into the somnambulant ear. They crouch
in the sand, squinting at grain-sized birds,
through the bruised-purple concord of dark algae, able
to fold like a wave of the sea.

In my envy, I will speak with the wind—
once I was high on the horn and drastic with music;
I made the slight widow shriek and the plump widow rage—

but that singular? That sure? That able to open a door?

AWAY NEAR THE DEAF SEA

Dawn was the frigate he took off on, his barge loaded
with bags of dry ice, leaving
me, a tintype, scrimshaw, sketch on the shore.

He went away to the deaf sea, its soft
limestone ruins, to seek the most immaculate
glaciers. He went away, bloodless
as the hemorrhage icebergs suffer: brooding
on stone, slid beneath the ship, deafened

by an avalanche, untuned to white noise. Immune
to night's stilted saxophone, he made sure not
to drown, scratching moonslate with his
tread. He struck

seared water, his arms
like matchsticks stiffened the current, his hissing
hookyards of tongue, the broken picket in his mouth,
the drifting body no one found.

I never heard him go,
but from the pitching bottom of the sea,
he took a tiny ruin
and put it in my hand.

RECENT TITLES FROM ALICE JAMES BOOKS

ALICE JAMES BOOKS has been publishing exclusively poetry since 1973. One of the few presses in the country that is run collectively, the cooperative selects manuscripts for publication through both regional and national annual competitions. New authors become active members of the cooperative, participating in the editorial decisions of the press. The press, which historically placed an emphasis on publishing women poets, was named for Alice James, sister of William and Henry, whose fine journal and gift for writing went unrecognized within her lifetime.

TYPESET AND DESIGNED BY MIKE BURTON

PRINTED BY THOMSON-SHORE